CO-CREATION

Partnering with God

An Artist's Journey

Alice Arlene Briggs

ISBN: 978-1-948666-008
Published by Alice Arlene, Ltd. Co.
P.O. Box 94825
Lubbock, TX 79493
books@alicearlene.com

It started with an observation.
It felt like God
was pleased
with me
in a different way
when I was painting
than
any other time.

I experimented.
What would increase
that sense of
God's pleasure?

I discovered that I could
intentionally seek His face
while I painted.
And I began to Partner with God.

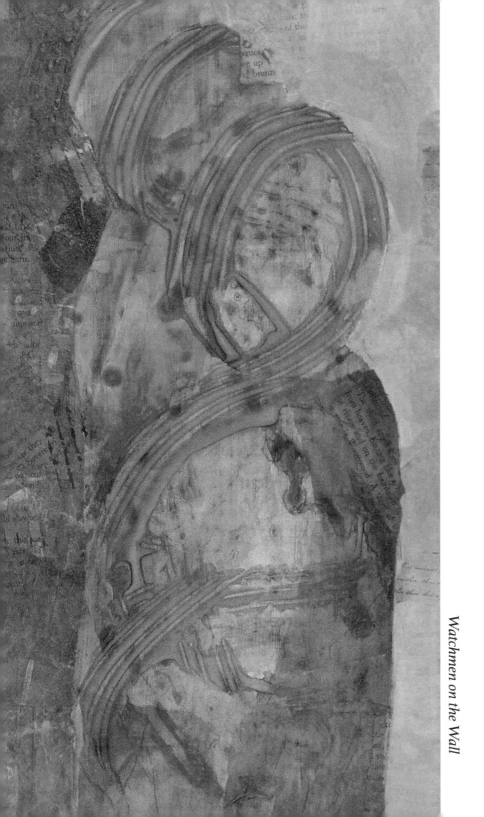

Watchmen on the Wall

Art Journey

For the last 25 years or more, my painting style has been to play with layers of paint and collage. I work intuitively and usually couldn't tell you why I put something in a particular place. It's not a logical process. I'm not pursuing a specific goal or image at any time.

Having minimal control over the process is a perfect place to set aside

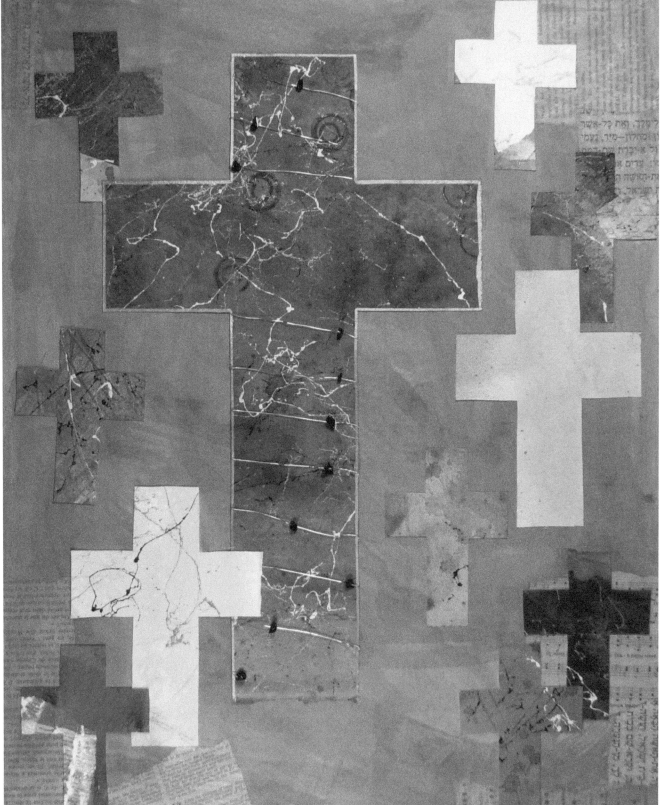

Glory of the Cross

my rational thought and logical thinking, and just create. It was in that place that I discovered a sense of God's pleasure like never before. He met me in the midst of creating. Not at the end, when there was a finished product, but in the mess and the chaos of the process. It was a rather startling revelation and one that began to transform my view of God and myself.

Hope

Beautiful Tenacity

Covenant Guardian

Ascent to the Gate

In the early creative days, I generally listened to music or podcasts while painting. My hands were busy doing something and I was usually in the same place for a while, so it gave me something to think about. I began to notice a difference in the creative process depending on what I was hearing. I began to experiment. I didn't do so formally, which I regret a bit now. It would be interesting to have documented what I tried and when and what resulted. But, alas, I have to rely on my memory and general impressions.

Encountering God

I wondered what would happen if I intentionally set out to encounter God while I was painting. If I consciously played the kind of music that spoke to my heart and soul the most while I was working, what would happen? What happened is that I began to feel closer to the Creator as I was creating than I did almost any other time. There grew a richness and a depth in our relationship that wasn't

San Pietro Cloisters

Assisi Gate

"I began
to feel
closer
to the
Creator
as I was
creating"

there before and was, amazingly, reflected in my work.

Playing worship music seemed to work the best, and I wondered if there was a difference in live versus recorded music. Because painting is a messy business, or at least I'm quite good at making a big mess, I had to modify my technique a bit. I took a sketchbook and colored pencils sometimes, and other times, I took collage materials and thicker glue and did mini collages in my lap. I found there wasn't a lot of difference, at least for me, in the creative process whether I was listening somewhere in person, listening via live webcast, or to previously recorded music.

Angel Trio

Prophetic Art

About this time, I started hearing about "Prophetic Art." I understood what they were doing, and the significance, but there was a disconnect in my mind between what I saw, and what I was doing. My work was becoming more abstracted, while most of what I saw of others' work was very representational.

During my experimentation, I received several prophetic words related to my artwork. The first times, I didn't realize it until later. Many I didn't know how to process, but I did write them down to see what would

Resurrection

...high, omnipotent, good Lord...
You all praise, glory and honor
...of every blessing
...You alone, Most high, do they bel...
...d no man is worthy to pronounce
...our name
...raise be to You my Lord
...ith all Your creatures
...specially Messer Brother Sun
Who illuminates the day for us
And he is beautiful and radiant
...ith great splendor
And from You, Most high, bring s mean...

Praise be to You my Lord
For Brother Fire
Through him You enlighten the night
And he is fair and merry
And vital and strong,
Praise be to You my Lord
For our sister Mother Earth
Who nourishes and sustains us all
And brings forth divers fruits
...colored flowers and herbs
...to You my Lord
...who pardon grant
...for love
...bear our infirmity and tribulation
Blessed are those who live in peace
...Most high,
...be crowned.
...to You my Lord
...Bodily Death
...living man can flee
...who die in mortal...

I will not be afraid...
what can man do to me?
...emember your leaders, those who spoke to you the
of God; consider the outcome of their life, and imitate
faith. ...Je... Christ... the same yesterday and today
...forever. Do not be led away by diverse and strange
...ings... it is well for the heart to be strengthened by
...not by foods, which have not benefited their adher-
...We have an altar from which those who serve the
...have no right to eat. For the bodies of those animals
...blood is brought into the sanctuary by the high priest
...sacrifice for sin are burned outside the camp. So Jesus
...suffered outside the gate in order to consecrate the people
...gh his own blood. Therefore let us go forth to him
...de the camp, bearing abuse for him. For here we
...no lasting city, but we seek the city which is to come
...rough him then let us continually offer up a sacrifi...
...aise to God, that is, the fruit of lips that acknowled...
...ame. Do not neglect to do good and to share whi...
...have, for such sacrifices are pleasing to God.

Waiting for Orders

happen. Some I'm now beginning to understand and see manifest. But I'm still amazed at the unlikeliness of all of this.

I didn't set out to become "A Prophetic Artist." No, I was just playing around in my studio, and following the questions in my head, heart, and spirit. "I wonder what would happen if," is the question that's begun many wild

adventures resulting in delightful discoveries.
Images Developing

To summarize my process, I build up the surface of the piece with multiple layers of paint and collage. My goal is to get the board covered with about three coats of paint, each one not wholly covering the layer below, but by the end of those three, the entire board has at least one

Servant

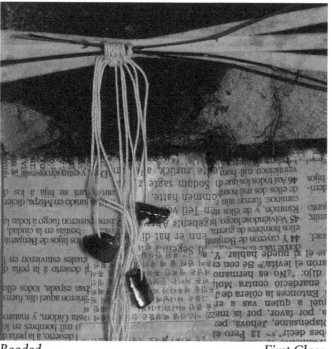

Beaded

Going Up

First Class

A Woven Key

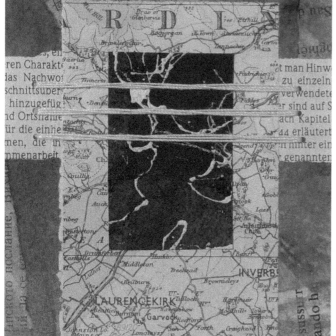

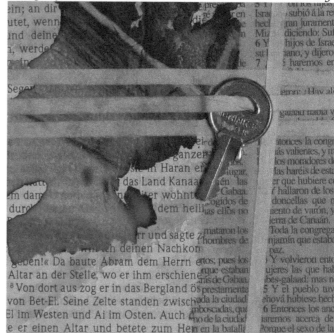

A few of those early "lap" collages.

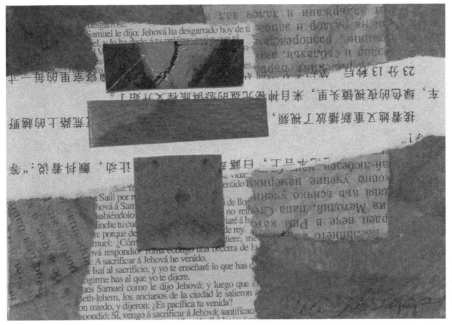

Springs Tree   Light of the World

layer of paint. I may then begin to collage or continue to add more and more color. I'm just playing and seeing what each layer is doing with the layers below. As I work, I sometimes find that an image begins to develop. A shape may appeal to me, or the layers will suggest a particular subject matter. I then decide how I will further develop my images.

Springs Door

Sometimes, words, phrases, and verses will come to mind while I work. When I am working on a personal prophetic piece, I make a note of those so I can be sure to include them in the prophetic word that will accompany the art piece to its new home. Often, it is the process that I am working on that seems significant so I will make a note of that as well. I general-

Angel

Sun Through the Trees

Burning Bush

ly don't know at the time what those things have to do with anything. And, sometimes, when I contemplate the piece after it is completed, I find that it was just something God was speaking to me during the process.

Message

For the Nation

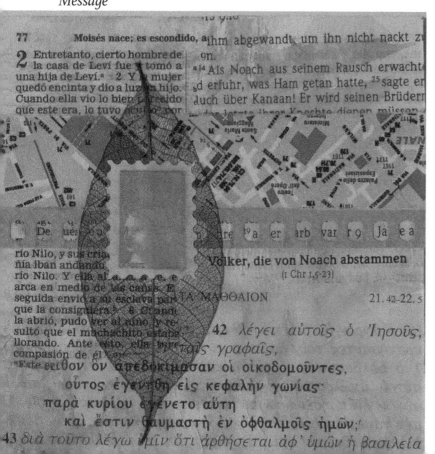

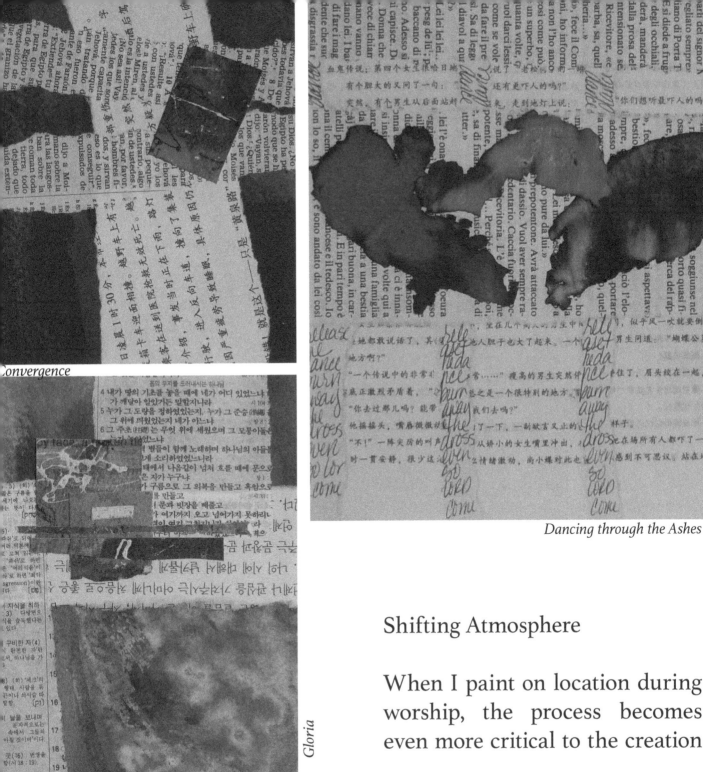

Convergence

Dancing through the Ashes

Gloria

Shifting Atmosphere

When I paint on location during worship, the process becomes even more critical to the creation of the piece. The production of the piece appears to shift the atmosphere, so others are freer to worship or to hear what God is speaking to them through the music and all that is happening. Those pieces are much less

Lilies

Windows

Secret Place

about the image than the process. Therefore, I am hesitant to "tweak" them later in the studio. Some are fairly good, and others are less so as far as the technical quality of work that I can produce. However, I'm learning to just let them be what they are.

I think my acceptance of imperfection of technique is essential. It's an entirely different thing to do a piece within an hour or two in front of people with all kinds of other activities happening than to complete a piece over the course of a few days in the studio with minimal distractions. Continuing to refine and hone my technique and skill level is very important to me, however. I find that the greater my level of skill or the development of my technique, the easier it is for me to express what I feel the Lord wants to convey in my work. It's a balance. Studio pieces and live worship ones are different and have a different purpose, or so I believe. Both are created with an intentional partnership with God, but while those created live are for those at the event, pieces in the studio may be part of my personal journey or about other people and places far away.

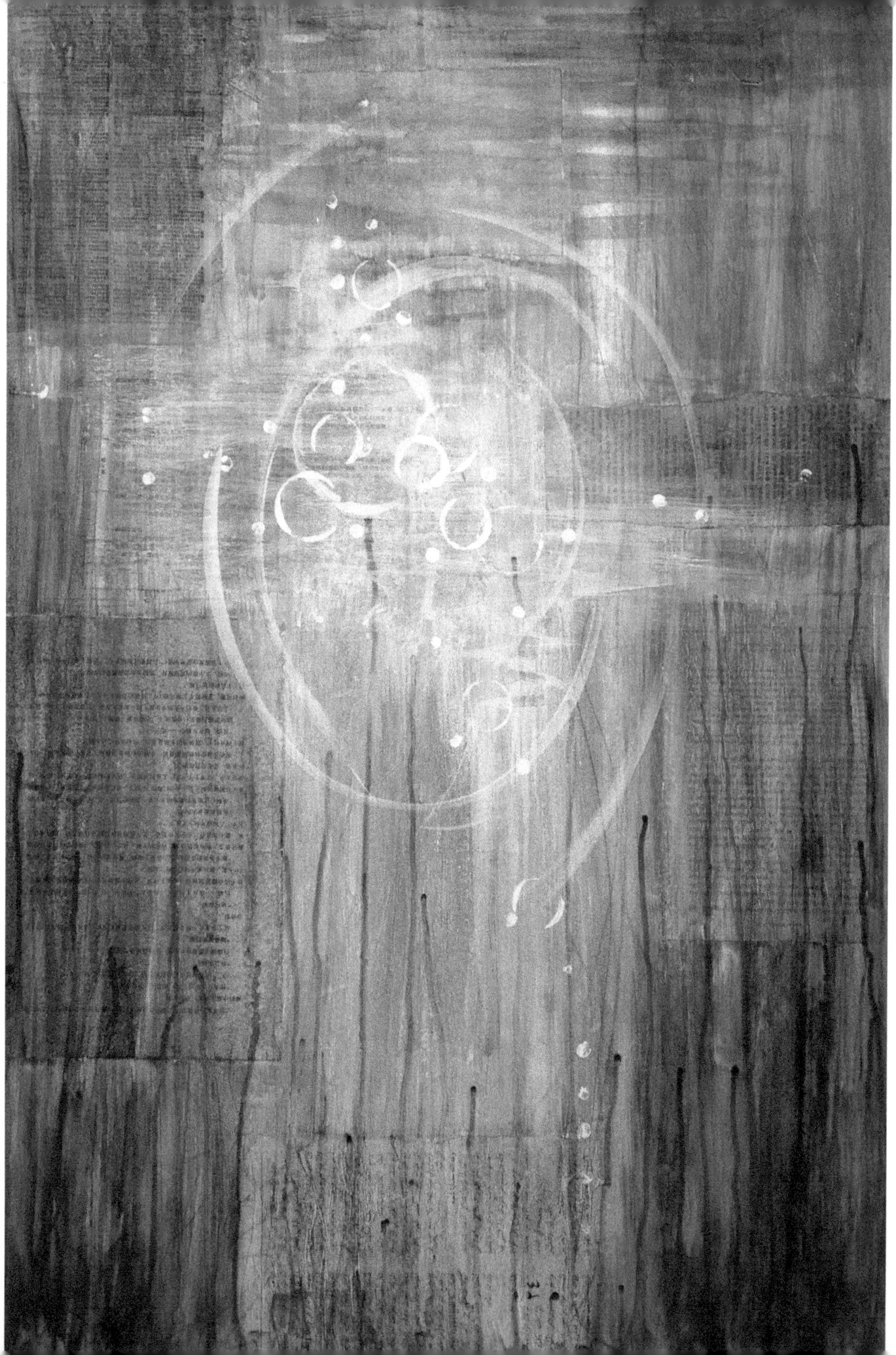

The Veil

Invitation to Explore

You'll notice as you read this book, that there are very few pieces with typical Christian imagery such as you see with much of the art that is called "prophetic." Angels show up from time to time, but even they

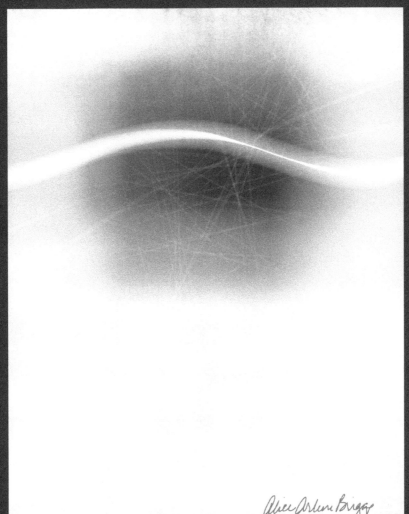

Peace

Alice Arlene Briggs

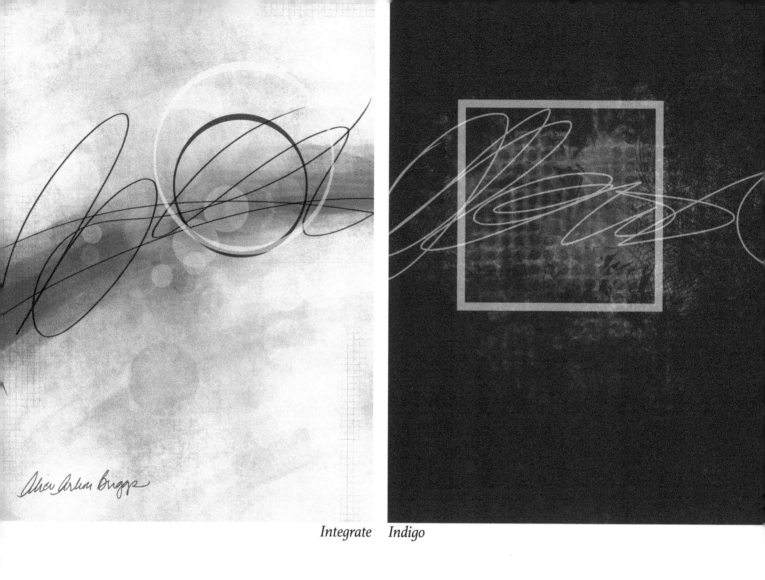

Integrate   Indigo

don't often look like what's typical. I've wondered about this, and I believe the Lord has shown me a couple of reasons. One is that those images, so far as art goes, are not something I've encountered a great deal until recent years. Another is that part of what I've always enjoyed the most about my work and people's responses to it is that it gets more in-

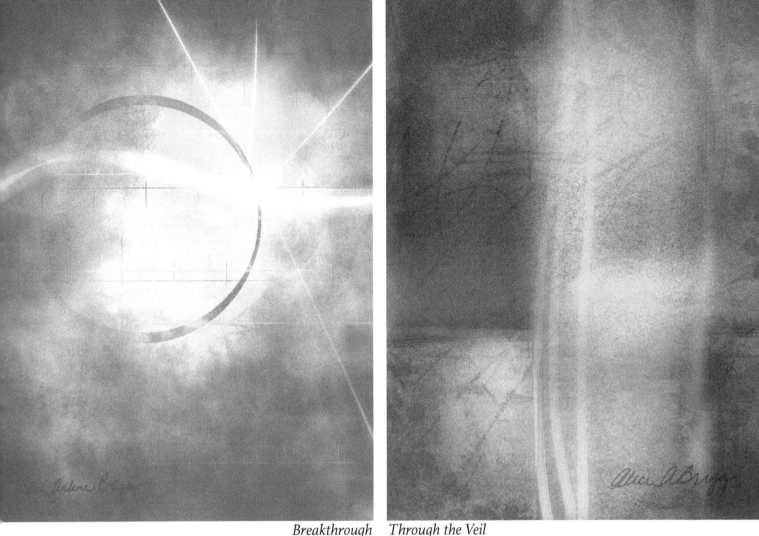

Breakthrough   *Through the Veil*

teresting the longer you look at it. You begin to see the collage materials peeking through the paint. You notice the textures and the layers of colors. It's an invitation to explore and experience. I don't want the piece to tell you what to think, I want you to hear and see for yourself. I want God to meet you where you are when you view my work.

Because of this, I've hesitated and struggled to provide people with "the meaning" of my work. I don't want to limit anyone to what I say or what the piece means to me. So, I nearly always give a disclaimer to listen for yourself and take the meaning that God gives you. However, I realized something about art historically. Art has often been a way to illuminate

Full Circle

Reset

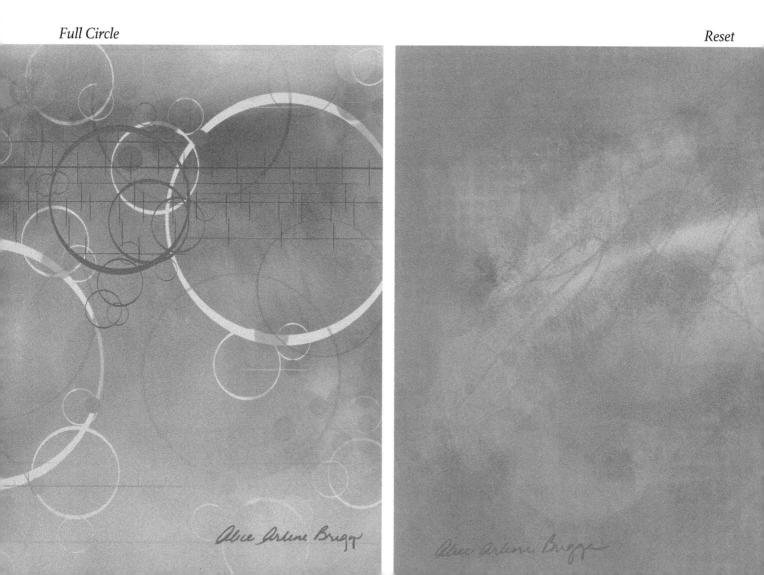

Alice Abriggs

and instruct people. For example, in the Middle Ages, paintings and sculpture were the only Bible most people could "read." Through those pieces, viewers were able to connect with the imagery of their faith.

Experiential Nature

With the Protestant Reformation, the church, in general, lost much of the mystical and experiential nature of Christianity that was an integral part of the early church. On the whole, we've been taught to study the Bible and learn without experiencing the One who wrote it. Don't get me wrong, I love a good Bible study and read it daily, but I've learned to read and study to hear, see, and experience, not just learn. I've discovered that the God of Abraham, Isaac, and Jacob wants to be the God of Alice and to lead her and speak with her and to give her solutions to her problems as He did with Moses, Joshua, Jesus, and Paul and continues to do with his people since those times.

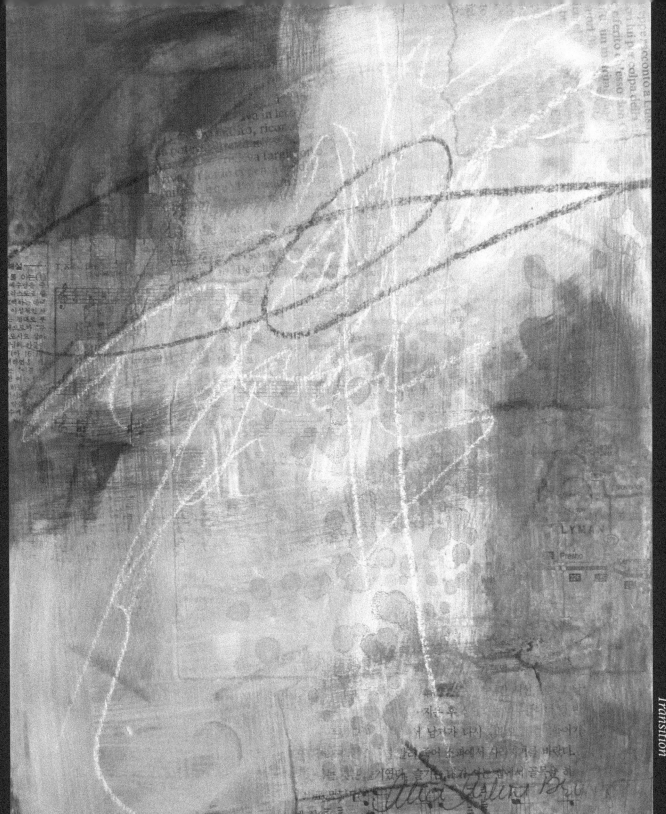

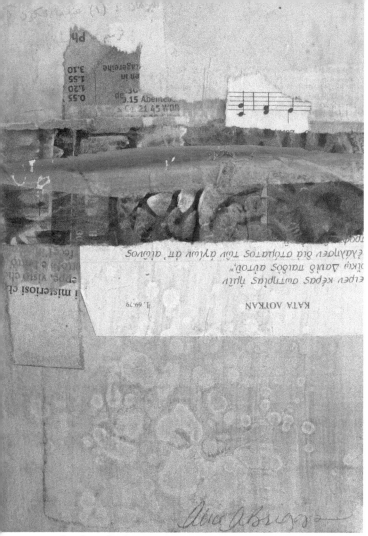

Ancient Ruins

Keep Moving Forward

Interpretation

Symbolism plays a significant role in determining the meaning of a piece. As I mentioned before, I make notes of anything that stands out to me while I create. Sometimes it's the overall color or the contrast of the colors that seems significant. Sometimes it's the textures or the shapes

that develop. More ob-
viously, are any words
or numbers that either
are in the collage mate-
rials or that I write on
the piece. If there's an
image, then that's an ob-
vious place to start, but
I generally find God has
more to say than what is
immediately apparent.
So, the best interpreta-
tions come from sitting
before Him and just lis-
tening to hear what He
would say while I con-
sider the piece.

As I journey down this
road, I begin to desire to
leave a trail that others
can follow. I can't speak

Foundations

"I've discovered that the God of Abraham, Isaac, and Jacob wants to be the God of Alice"

Glorious

for the artists great and unknown who left their mark on the cathedrals and churches across Europe, but I can imagine them intent on creating a piece that would enable viewers to experience the stories of the Bible profoundly. Similarly, my hope for my work is that it would leave breadcrumbs for viewers to follow and discover this great and awesome God who longs to meet each of us

Burning Ones   *Brigners of Gifts*

Veil

where we are and talk and walk with us throughout all that life throws at us.

As you linger over the images in this book - don't just seek to understand. Seek to feel and hear and experience the piece, and the God of all creation Who longs to meet you there. And then, begin to feel, hear, see, and experience Him throughout the rest of your day, week, and life.

Thank you for joining me on this adventure into partnering with God. I invite you to follow my further adventures via my website and blog at www.alicearlene.com; you can also find me on Facebook, Twitter, and Instagram @alicearleneb.

I would be happy to complete a personal prophetic piece just for you or a loved one. If you would like a print co-created in partnership with God delivered monthly to your home, I have subscriptions available. You can view these options, and other originals and prints, on my website at www.alicearlene.com.

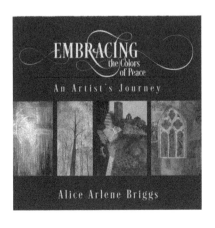

Join me on my adventures into emotional and spiritual expression through paint and collage. This book features work from my earliest explorations with my intuitive method until more recent works that Embrace the Colors of Peace.

Available on Amazon

Lightning Source UK Ltd.
Milton Keynes UK
UKHW020933100223
416696UK00003B/152